A WISHING-WELL
OF WORDS

Michèle Glazer

MINERVA PRESS

LONDON
ATLANTA MONTREUX SYDNEY

A WISHING-WELL OF WORDS
Copyright © Michèle Glazer 1998

ISBN 1 86106 190 8

First Published 1998 by
MINERVA PRESS
195 Knightsbridge
London SW7 1RE

Printed in Great Britain for Minerva Press

A WISHING-WELL
OF WORDS

Dedicated to:

my daughter, Diandra
a fairy muse in my life.

President Nelson Mandela
for his licensing of artistic
freedom in South Africa;

Lynette Allan, who valued
and encouraged my poetry.

My mother, Etty.
With grateful thanks to God!

Contents

Masquerade

Dedicated to the most genuine Queen – Diana, Princess of Wales
(and to the consciences of those who trod on her shadows).

I dreamed it was the springtime of my life again,
I lived on an expectant carousel
No triste yesterdays, lugubrious tomorrows
I was the Princess of Penistone Crag...

Why did you masquerade amour for me
Gesturing it all away, a wizard
Stealing my magic carpet in mid-flight?
Why did you allege you loved me...

Utopian, now sardonically sad
Every shadowy step an indifferent accomplishment,
With you I perceived I could glide
Like a unicorn on a dream...

The spasm of unrequited love
Plunders the wings from the most exquisite butterfly,
Binds the feet of the most vibrant of dancers
Reviles even a Princess's body on a torturer's rack;
That awesome Grecian Urn pales visibly!

Yet, I pledge these words so they may be
Infinitely potent, to warn of the wasted war zone
Of love unrequited and undeserved.
I humbly extend the strumming strands
Of help to experiences and their harbourers, everywhere.

This fragile silk tied in zigzags to memories... regrets?
A subtle trapeze artist reveals it strong enough
To balance on, walking backwards;
Or maybe forwards now...

Diana... your trapeze artist lost her balance...
Mais le vent sentira toujours ton parfum!

To Be African

Dedicated to President Nelson Mandela

My blood is not blue!
That which colours my veins
Is an untamed red.
Like the barren boulders
Naked rocks of the bush,
Reflecting a vermilion sun
The intensity that is Africa.

From lion cubs gambolling about
To predators roaming free
Even the people permanently possessed
By the spell of an African storm.
We do not take offence
When potent lightning, sovereign thunder
Splinters a landscape
Never before disturbed.
Bushfires, bare feet
Unconstrained laughter and pain;
A mystic mist, Africa's soul
Lilting over all.

Her enigma does not extend
To the parts where the Nile flows;
A mistake joined by a magnet,
Pieces of a puzzle that do not fit.
For, when the stars flirt with your eyebrows
On a quiet Bushveld night
An incomparable aura ordains,
Elevates you to where
No one else will ever reach.

When the dusk sun
Fingers the rugged mountain shapes
And the moon rises from the plains,
I am infused with pride
For the single segment of earth
That can never be contained.

A Love Unaccomplished

Dishevelled hair,
your riddle of a face
grinding morning cereal.

Watching you for so many years
the same chair no closer now;
I, the daughter, always the stranger.

Why threat or foe when so dear to me?
Deformed love, close to hatred;
not your own, from past generations.

Pursed lips, sarcastic teeth
eyes afraid of my own outlining
the shape of a rumour unrevealed.

In an attic (escape from me)
your fugitive fingers agitate a weary cello
hidden from a beckoning funeral gown.

When morbid grey glances over
your features in your frugal resting place,
anger, regret at my impenetrable love for you.

Adieu, mother!
Your broken haircomb will always
put me to sleep.

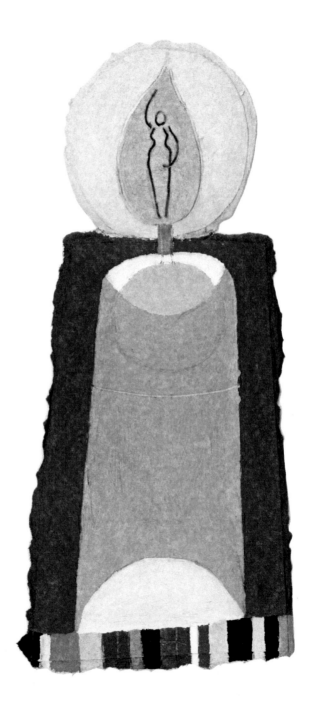

To All Artists

Dedicated to the incomparable
Rudolph Nureyev and Margot Fonteyn

A soprano ravishes with notes
As you alight from so transient a plane,
In so fleeting a form.
That unsullied, rousing imprint in time
When you compose a superlative
Finer than dewdrops on a spider's web!

What outlines your form
Apart from others, alienating you
From rampant receptiveness
That should be your constant crown?
Where is the wax from hallowed candles
Dispersing perpetual bouquets at your feet?

For some, your allure wanes
When gravity and age attempt to woo
You from your interminable plane.

For me, your design is timeless!
Feeding the camera images in my mind
With immortal influence... and solace.

The Leopard Stalks Oblivion

What will there be for
Pending generations to see?
Discarded railway tracks;
An ocean green with slime,
Patterns of litter on tedious streets
With a sky chain-smoking heavily.

We are the last for whom
The early morning light will
Daub her temperate colours
On a discernible canvas.
How will I sketch the acorn's
Formidable heap of promise
Or willows lapping water
With green, grateful tongues,
When it will be so rare to see
Any seat in soil unblemished
By measles of humanity?

The images in my crystal conjuror
Show a dispirited hermit crab
Combing currents for a solitary, sanitary shell;
A distraught wind seeks signs of
Formerly familiar imprints in sand.
The roar of a lion rambles along

The peaks of Kilimanjaro, impotent
To repossess its path. The velvet grace of
The leopard stalks the defection of the dodo.

A handful lead by torch and tread
With steps resonating respect:
They are grains of desert sand
Attempting to build a pyramid.

Sombre Love

Sometimes in the dance
Even the slick slide of our necks
Trace the same shape;
Hushed harmony from the lines
Of a perfect *pas de deux*
Curtain calls... bouquets.

Sometimes the hands of an old clock
Your body's staggered response to mine;
Moody *coupées*, reticent arabesques
Limp lines lost in time.

Then... the desperate *dégagées*;
Oh, release Ophelia from her Fate
For Hamlet shall never
Love her!

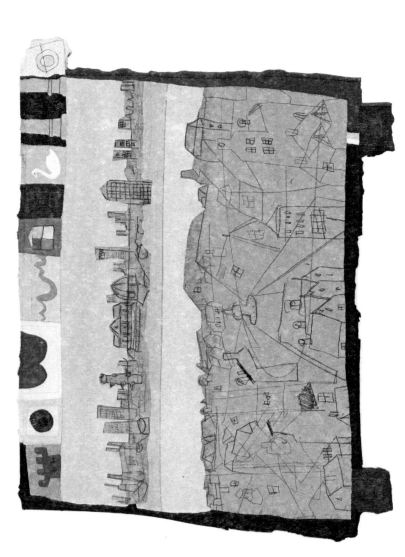

My London

Princess swathed in lilac-grey silk,
In all the rooms of your castle, you –
Like a jack-in-the-box – surprise me,
Inspire me; swelling my reality
With dance, music, art, theatre,
Bohemian oddities;
Satisfied to be singular.

Queen of the eclectic, your
Classically trained fingers
Lead to Rock arm movements;
A torso decorated by Modern,
Monet and Manet; breasts
Moulded to the deviant lines
Of trendy furniture; your private
Parts regally reserved for Soho.

Lithe legs lend finesse to ballet
The eccentric and all that is nouveau,
Tips of manicured toenails do not
Disappoint your rambling lawns
And museums. Glistening in
Sun-gold for those ballroom
Appearances, your neck and Venus-like
Face resemble the swans

21

On your lucid lakes; multifaceted
Visions of all beauty.

When Big Ben sings out the twelve notes
Of midnight, the romance
And adventure have just begun.

The Lady of the Lake

When the early morning's whispers
Ruffle my curtains, I identify you
Untainted and opaque;
The autobiography of a matchless dimension
On which I labour to live...

So stirring in purity, recherché
On the material level, you gleam
Through the water in a soporific smile –
An intimation of the Garden of Eden,
How the essence was meant to be.

Swan, do not refrain from reaching;
Do not waver on the waves
Or turn from the current's ardent arms
We are artfully adjoined here,
Yet will soon be universally united...

Ballad for Lost Lovers

Disdain is dead!
Burning curses the restrained
Refrains of a high requiem,
Will they here
Sweetly sing soft songs?

Thrushes trilled on the
Opening buds, butterflies
Blended to the stirring waltz;
They did not whisper
The mouth-watering melody.

When the sun slept longer
To the moon's lullaby
O, the despondent slide
Of their tepid tango.
Death, will you
Inspire a divine duet?

Progress and the Moon

The night is pubescent
The new moon incandescent;
The innocence of a child's face
Softly etched on her transparent blush.
Fairies frolic under a garland of stars
Winged wonders whisper
Across a spellbound sky;
The moon's serenity disturbed
Only by a smile with her eyes
Before this ethereal energy.

A fuller moon, an adolescent night,
Satellites trespass her broader vision
Microchip clichés lure her wider eyes;
Fairies fade into farewells
Electric antagonism infiltrates her orbit.
Her complexion, pallid as a latex mask,
Contorts with confusion.

Then again, she is the new moon
Magically mounted on to the stillness
Of the night; the sole satellites, falling stars
Conjuring up clouds of cascading contours.
The trace of a smile is again
Part of her allure.

We can never turn back!

Fresh Blossoms

The hurt flares out, I endure
Your pain, like a heater
Against the brain. I become
An agonised, antagonised lioness.

Destruction, be pall-bearer to
Those who compel the fresh
Blossoms to wilt for you!

Yet, your love excels, for
You are so young that
Conjuring plastic surgeons deftly
Remodel those, who should be
Restrained as gravel in the tar,
Of a road leading nowhere.

Brother?

I scrape the match beside the tears
In my dress; light reflects into cushions
And corners interpreting prosperity,
Christmas with your family.

You turn and smile and I recognise
Those teeth you shaped before
My girlish eyes; a trace too sharp –
I should have been cautioned, brother.

I could not have conceived it would be
You, for grubby affluence, your muse
The repetitious imprint of some
President's profile. I should never
Have pretended it would not be you!

The river that teased us as children
Rushes in tears, wipes her eyes
On bark ingrained with our initials.
What mask will you wear
When you spurn my fading flame?

Shafts of light glimpse the sores on fingers
That will never form scabs and heal;
My wristwatch monitors seconds that
Blind the minutes from the bolt
Of shocking shades of truth.

Heathcliff, when your kindred Cathy
Scratches on your windowpane,
Will you allow her in – or
Will those marks haunt as
Your fingerprints at the scene of a crime?

The Highwayman

I am too absorbed for
The telling tick-tock
Of Time and clock
Pilfering precious moments
With no thought or guile?
Ensnared by each instant,
He turns over the chapters of my life
Before I am braced
To face and see
What will there be?

And then my child is born;
I stroke her silent skin
Caress her calmness
Claim her close;
Hankering for the halt
Of the candour of the clock
The indifference of passing hours,
The years that will rob me of her.

Is Time innocent
In tiptoeing away
With what is so nonpareil?
Or is he a highwayman
In disguise, premeditating
Our lives and our demise?

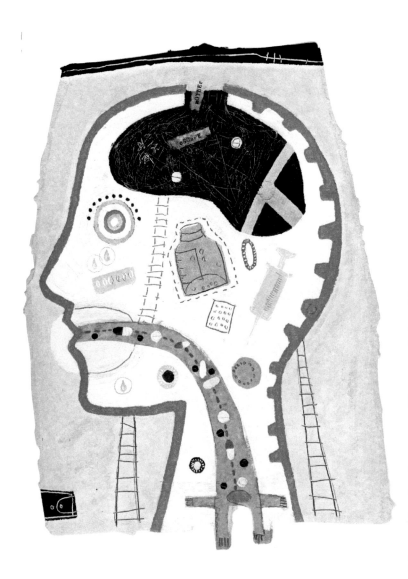

Tears No Longer Flow

Pills or pethidine modify
Response from our souls.
Beta blockers bridle emotions,
Once wild stallions inhaling incense
From friendly grass around hooves,
Horseshoed from the fervent earth.

Mother, why do tears
Never streak your face?
When moisture threatens
Fragile flesh on all sides of eyes,
Drops stagger, stutter out over the
Shattered shroud of a dated accessory.

Feelings forced out, child
Only through shocked doses of
Heroin, cocaine; momentary contact
With a deeper intuition... slipping into oblivion.

I do not feel these lines jotted down
From so deep a void unveiled.

Wait, tears babble out;
I am free, I am me!

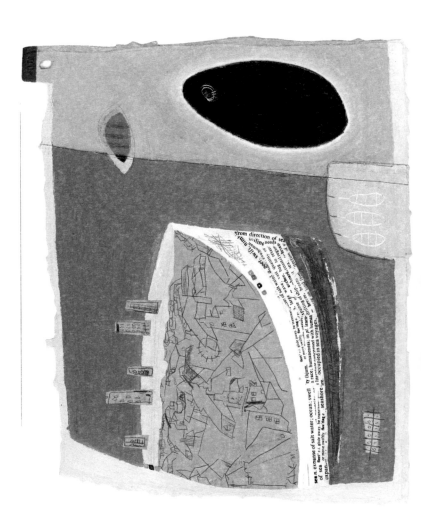

sea n. expanse of salt water; ocean; swell
of sea ~ a tide away by tra~~~ seashore ~c.
captain~ or move swiftly for ing c

My Retreat to the Sea

When I returned from the sea...
From waves in pillows of foam
Drawn into emerald, overlapping into blue;
The perfumed smell survived
The sweet-toned sound lingered on.
Ailing , jaded elegies from humanity
Hushed for a while.

Even the sullen, grey walls
Fleetingly masked by flawless designs.

Serenade

A flower's birth in the soothing sun,
Serenading with its rays of light
To the flute for the newborn buds.
From where does this bleakness appear,
Like a cadaverous mask
Disguising all hints of hope?
Where is the melodious light
That persistently basked its way through?

Cold, calculated concrete casts its callous
Mould on a harmonious landscape
Of plants and patterns, pulsating pictures
In alluring shades and textures
Now concealed from the rising sun.

More and more sombre
Light forces its way through,
Only to trace steely structures
Against a fractured landscape;
What is this sword that severs
Our umbilical bond with earth, light and harmony?

A Memory to my Father

Every snowflake floating to the ground
Remains intact... briefly,
Vanishing into fluid, digested by soil
Omitted unremittingly!
You select a deviating destiny,
Inspirited into our present
So teardrops are too fulfilled to fall.

In a Moonlit Cask

Like a candle in the darkness
Stirred by each mood of the wind,
My senses will measure each murmur of ocean
With the beat of your heart.

I saw that esoteric ship edge past
When your feelings were enmeshed in my bones,
Wooden with silver lights, augmenting
The promise of the moon.

How can I induce you to hold destiny's hands
When you slip onto a diverted path –
Psychics, astrology or Divine intervention?
It hurts like a needle
Plunging into a boil!

Shall we escort the heirs of the Montagues
And Capulets... hardly a curtsey
Or bow to earth's symphony,
Before bonding, ebbing eternally?

The galleon spectre reappears with a cask
Furrowed by veins of moonlight;
It is our time now, we dare
Not evade our fate; your heart
Pulsating with mine in a moonlit cask.

The flares of Her Holy Lighthouse
Chaperoning our path...

Our House at the Sea

Buttercup walls befriend no spiders' webs
here, entanglements of a different nature.
They could have encircled much gaiety
vivid wallpaper matching the blouse
she wore when they led her away.

From the balcony a postcard
of the sea in varying moods,
confusion among the dice
in the box of the board game,
keyholes whisper of my own lost life;
if only I did not see so much of yesterday.

Our 'secret garden' remembers laughter
with vivid rose brambles,
palm trees peep over lavender
winking at our African roots
so close to where the two oceans meet.

The mangled fly screen blocks flies and feelings,
disdainful kitchen tiles smell of fish.
The doll looks benignly from the bay window;
she held her whenever dusk began
to conceal the harshness of day.
The scarlet curtain tones in with her lipstick,
the flag to the bull of abuse she incited!

The house is tranquil after many yearning years;
I always saw beyond your eyes.
I know the scarlet curtain remembers!

Adieu

Dismally, slowly
disperses the dream
under a crowd
of lifeless autumn leaves.
The memory edges away
but, there will forever
be a deep, damp sneer
where the leaves once lay,
(now blown away)
in my heart.

Hunter

You may remove an African from the bush
You may never disembowel the bush
From an African!

In aching sun, lioness and cubs
Seem painted in the sienna and umber tones
Of grasses, nudged to surrender
Their places momentarily, before
Pliably stretching back into shape.
Steam contours vapour hearts
From the waterhole, like a kettle
Wooing air amorously.

An oddity appears on the vast terrain
Ornate in red and gold, new socks
Sunblock (with an outsized hat)
Dwelling on a receding jawline,
Viciously chewing gum.

The perceptive eyes of Marula trees stare,
The nostrils of animals, disdainfully startled,
Twinge unnoticed a few footprints away;
The hunter suckles a bottle of gin
And howls at thorns confronting his socks.

A skeleton of mangled meat is placed
In the reluctant grass, to orphan!
The credulous , mangy lioness spots
The maroon aura for cubs cutting teeth.
Orange eyes against wheaty grass
Lured by the red of it all.

A shot hushes the stillness...
The drugged lioness wavers;
The killer, intimidated by the flaccid
Debilitated body he has inflicted upon her,
Panics; is entertained whilst plunging
Six bullets into the still elegant, slipping form.

Six bullets, six seconds that shatter!
I am African... I will compulsively care,
My soul is never far away from there.
Beware... when your prey is ethically equipped,
You will face the vindicating frown
Of atomic ammunition.

Realms of Reality

For my daughter, Diandra

No one can ever wrest away
From me those treasured times
That I can see
When I close my eyes
And life becomes young;
When you danced through the air
With your smile, for a while.
And oh, the mermaids we could see
With dolphins dancing in harmony;
Knights in castles
Lollipops and lavender
Your candy-flossed face,
After a day to embrace.

And then I brood over why
To so many men
The stars are just diamonds
The ground hard and gold
The grass money per metre
The impoverished in the cold
When we would thrill to feel all
The secrets in the ocean's shawl.

I uncover my eyes and cannot see
That you were only lent to me.
The truth will not just be
The awesome actuality
Of high-risers levitating
Into their high-rises,
Pushing lift buttons
Towards a pre-empted future.
Their routes cast in black tar
Under the wheels of a garish motor car.

Yet, our years together vanished
On the glint of a sunbeam;
Our time seems as transient
As the twinkle of morning dew.
But, that one pensive penny I can see
Given with your love to me,
Is now a field of blooming blossoms
Moulded in my mind.
Your sylph-like silhouette
Sifts through the air,
Any time... any where.

Africa's Bush

by Diandra Glazer, 7 years old

When the lion stalks his prey
The bush keeps still;
When the hippos go underwater
Everything is startled,
When the zebra trots
All the stripes cover the bush.

When the spotted eagle flies
The song fills the air. The hyena laughs,
The other animals flee,
When the moon shines
Brighter than the stars.